Teaching Strategies
& Techniques
for Adjunct Faculty

Sixth Edition

Donald Greive, Ed.D.

Order Information:

Part-Time Press
P.O. Box 130117
Ann Arbor, MI 48113-0117
www.Part-TimePress.com
PH   734-930-6854
ISBN 13-digit 978-0-940017-43-6

Printed in the United States of America

& Techniques

PREFACE

With the ever increasing numbers of part-time and adjunct faculty teaching today, institutions are assuming more responsibility for providing support and assistance to them. The expertise and experience of part-time faculty are becoming increasingly important to students and institutions. This expertise, however, can only be adequately appreciated if it is recognized and incorporated into the instructional process.

This book has been prepared specifically to assist adjunct faculty, many of whom will have careers outside of education, in efficiently grasping concepts necessary for effective teaching.

Realizing the time constraints facing part-time faculty who choose to share their experience and expertise in the classroom, this book is intentionally brief and to the point. Individuals interested in examining the teaching process in greater detail may find the companion publication, *A Handbook for Adjunct/Part-time Faculty and Teachers of Adults*, of value. It is the hope of the author and publisher that, in some small way, this publication will assist faculty in achieving a successful and rewarding teaching experience.

Donald Greive, Ed.D.

CONTENTS

& Techniques

INTRODUCTION

This book has been written to efficiently present teaching strategies and techniques. It is purposely brief to provide *teaching faculty a quick and straightforward reference. Most of the topics discussed here are covered in greater depth in *A Handbook for Adjunct/Part-time Faculty and Teachers of Adults*.

As an adjunct faculty member, you make a significant contribution to your institution and to the students who take your classes. Regardless of your reason for teaching, your effectiveness will depend upon the amount of preparation you devote as a teacher. If you are new or returning to the classroom after being away, you will find that student expectations of college instruction continue to change and evolve. You'll find this book full of tips, strategies, and proven techniques that address face-to-face teaching in the college classroom making your teaching experience productive and enjoyable. So let's get on with it...

* For the purposes of this publication the terms teaching, adjunct and part-time faculty are used interchangeably.

Who am I????

... A part-time faculty member!

If I'm early, no one notices ...

... If I'm late, everyone does.

If I'm well-prepared for 101 ...

... I'm assigned 102.

If I have 25 handouts prepared ...

... there are 26 in the class.

If I'm well-prepared...

... the class is cancelled.

If I'm under-prepared ...

... 53 students register.

As a part-time faculty member, I am invaluable! In fact, in some institutions I am responsible for 50 percent or more of the total credit hours taught. I teach anytime, any section, any students. Often, I teach after a full day of work. Equally as often, I bring real-world skills, energy and expertise to the institution where I teach.

Why do I teach? I want to share my experience, talents, and skills with others; I want to help bridge the gap between the academic world and the surrounding community; I want to explore new frontiers of learning, and I love teaching.

 Check for the KEY icon when reading this booklet. The KEY is used to highlight special techniques and key concepts to improve your teaching.

FACULTY CHECKLIST

So, you've accepted a position as an adjunct faculty member, received your class assignment, and signed your contract. Listed below are some points you'll want to review with your supervisor prior to beginning your first day of class. Add additional items to create your own personal checklist.

1. Have I completed all my paperwork for employment?
2. Is there a department course syllabus, course outline, or statement of goals and objectives available for the course?
3. How do I get a copy of the text, e-text and any ancillary materials for teaching the class?
4. When are grades due and when do students receive grades?
5. Is there a college and/or departmental grading policy?
6. Is there training for the college's Learning Management System?
7. Are there prepared department tests?
8. What are the library's print and electronic use and Internet policies and procedures?
9. What instructional aids are available?
10. What IT support is available to faculty?
11. Is there a college and/or department attendance or tardiness policy?
12. Where can I get instructional aid materials such as audio or visual materials, etc., and what is the lead time for ordering?
13. What are the names of the department chairperson, dean, department secretaries, learning resource and support staff, and other significant college officials and how can I reach them, if needed?
14. Have course objectives been reviewed to incorporate the most appropriate technology?
15. Who are some of the other faculty who have taught the course and are they open to assisting adjuncts?

GETTING STARTED

Learning is best accomplished when there is a desire to learn and when it builds on prior learning and knowledge. So true learning is as much the responsibility of the student as the teacher. Teachers, however, are an integral part of the learning process and require certain professional skills and competencies. Individuals can no more expect to walk in front of a class without these skills and excel, than one could expect to walk into the middle of an engineering project or legal case and succeed.

The critical difference between teaching and other professions is quite simple. Most professions are very content-oriented, requiring an adequate mastery of subject and a considerable amount of hard work to succeed. In the world of teaching, those factors—while necessary—are useless without possessing the ability to communicate with other human beings.

The basic characteristics of good teaching are:
- **Knowing one's subject**
- **Being able to communicate it effectively**
- **Knowing and liking students**
- **Understanding one's culture**

Student Characteristics

College faculty encounter few certainties; however, one certainty is that you will face increasingly diverse groups of students. Their backgrounds and aspirations are significantly different from those of the typical "college student" from decades ago. You must be constantly alert to stereotyping students or classes since it diminishes your chances of success with the group.

Listed below are five common characteristics that may be found in today's college students:

1. College students will have a better grasp of where they are going and why they are in class. They may become frustrated if their expectations are not met.
2. College students may view themselves as consumers as well as students. They feel they have purchased a product and they will expect its delivery.
3. They will come to class more mature and more open to sharing their rich life experiences. Many times these experiences can be a valuable asset to the class.
4. They are adults and expect to be treated as such. Very often, adult students will rebel at rules and standards that do not seem to contribute to the learning process.
5. Many students have grown up in a culture driven by the immediacy of Instagram, email and the Internet. This may encourage attitudes of disrespect as well as comparisons to professional performers.

To challenge these students, instructors need to develop active learning teaching strategies and experiential activities such as think-pair-share, cooperative learning, quick writes and other activities in which students assume responsibility for themselves and their peers.

Classroom Communication

As pointed out earlier, the principal ingredient of professional teaching is the ability to communicate clearly. In a classroom, communication is more than talking and lecturing. Communication involves eye contact, physical gestures, classroom presence and proper media and blackboard usage.

Become acquainted with cultural nonverbal communication indicators and, above all, be conscious of any traits that may be construed as offensive or distracting to students. At the same time, be conscious of your strengths. Reflect upon your most positive features and mannerisms and incorporate them into your teaching strategies.

And finally, *remember that the three R's of teaching are repeat, respond, and reinforce.* This means that student comments and contributions, if worthy of mention, are worthy of being repeated, responded to and reinforced by the verbal and nonverbal techniques at the command of the teacher.

STRATEGIES FOR TEACHING

You should have in your repertoire a variety of approaches to teaching. The following are some important concepts and strategies that have received considerable attention in teaching/learning circles during the past decade.

Andragogy/Pedagogy

With the recent rise in the number of adults attending college, teaching experts have recognized that these new learners bring with them different expectations about their role in the learning process. In fact, it is evident that adults want to play a more active role in their learning experience. In the past, most of us were placed in classes where the teacher determined the activities needed to achieve learning, making the teacher the center of the instructional process. This is called pedagogy and is a vital part of the teaching process. However, experts have realized that pedagogy does not work for all learners in all situations.

Contemporary learners, especially adults, want to be more active in their education. Specifically, they want to know why they must learn something prior to undertaking it; they possess a strong sense of self and feel responsible for their own decisions; and they wish to integrate their life and employment experiences into their learning activities. *These factors influenced the creation of a learner-centered strategy known as andragogy.*

For you as an instructor, the implications are very clear. Your classroom preparation should include learner-centered activities. Many such activities are included here but are not labeled as such.

Remember, however, that the andragogical model does not imply that the pedagogical model should be abandoned. There is still a need for pedagogical planning tempered by the concepts and strategies of andragogy.

Developing an andragogical teaching strategy requires a classroom that fosters open communication. Be aware that some adults may be anxious about their ability to learn, so plan activities that build student confidence and provide opportunities for students to share their experiences. You must establish yourself as a partner in learning and not an expert who has all of the answers.

 Teaching experts increasingly acknowledge that *students learn from each other as much as from their instructors.* Working together improves all students' achievement in the classroom.

Five important student-centered teaching strategies are experiential learning, cooperative or collaborative learning, partnering, classroom assessment technique, and feedback mechanisms.

Experiential Learning

Experiential learning is also referred to as experiential teaching, or experiential training and development, or experiential activities, and other variations of these terms (Thompson 2013). However the word, learning, is significant since it emphases the learner's perspective, which is crucial to the experiential learning concept. Conversely, the words training and teaching, significantly reflect the teacher or training perspective (on behalf of the teaching or training organization—e.g., a school or employer).

The phrase experiential learning and development are achieved through personal experience and involvement, rather than on received teaching or training, typically in group, by observation, listening, study of theory or hypothesis, or some other transfer of skills or knowledge.

Experiential learning, especially used at the beginning of a person's new phase of learning, can help to provide a positive emotional platform for future learning, even for areas of learning which initially

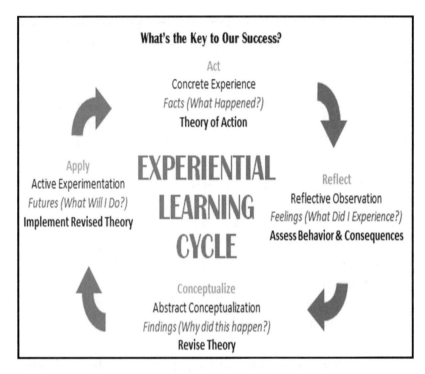

would have been considered uncomfortable or unnecessary.

Experiential learning also brings into play the concept of multiple intelligences - the fact that people should not be limited by the 'three Rs' and a method of teaching based primarily on reading and writing.

Experiential learning is a way to break out of training and teaching practices which have constrained people's development in schools and work. Here are the principles of experiential learning:

1. **It's about them—not you**: As an effective facilitator, you have to be satisfied with the knowledge that you offer and develop opportunities for others to learn, many of which will go unused or undervalued.

2. **Resist temptation to give answers—ask questions only**: Don't tell people what they should learn. An observer is in a privileged position, often seeing aspects that are not obvious to others. What-

ever happens, don't be tempted to provide a 'professional analysis' as this approach takes the ownership of the learning away from the individual.

3. **Accentuate the positives**: It is all too easy to focus on the negatives but this can seriously undermine confidence in the whole idea of learning and development if the negatives are over-emphasized.

4. **Learner is central**: Learners have to be prepared to actively develop their understanding, critique and evaluate the messages in their context and then work hard to apply appropriate learning.

5. **Facilitation must be light and subtle**: Experiential learning involves students working things through for themselves and developing their own understanding. Facilitators should always be seeking ways to enable this to happen.

6. **Find/create experiential learning opportunities**: A facilitator should help create learning opportunities and enable others to recognise and make good use of these opportunities.

7. **Reactions to experiences vary, so don't prejudge**: Because individuals are personally involved in experiential learning, individuals can take very different messages from a single event. Therefore one event can provide the students involved with quite different or even diametrically opposed reactions.

8. **Careful reviews of activities are crucial**: The learning review is a vital stage of every activity. It should be planned as part of the design, not left to chance. Reviews can take many forms but all must engage the learners. The ideal review will involve the learner in personal thought, challenge and discussion before coming to a conclusion. It is often useful if a period of individual reflection, guided by open-ended or tick-box questionnaires, is followed by a facilitated discussion. If it is to be of

real benefit, the review must be an honest critique of what happened and the contributions of each individual. Real issues should not be swept under the carpet, but equally criticism must be constructive.

Cooperative Learning

Sometimes called collaborative learning, this strategy brings students with differing abilities together in small groups where they reinforce lecture and text material through interaction and discussion. This technique requires detailed planning, including classroom goals, specific activities, and a grading plan. Groups should consist of four or five students. During this activity, the instructor assumes the role of facilitator, maintaining direction and assuring complete student participation.

A good cooperative learning group is established with several conditions. You must make sure all students participate, have a method to capture individual student's participation, and require a tangible result from the group activity.

> The benefits of cooperative learning include:
> * students have a vehicle to get to know others in the class (very important for part-time students),
> * students develop a commitment to the group,
> * grades improve,
> * out-of-class group study is encouraged, and
> * students become participants in their own learning.

Partnering

 Some instructors find that *assigning students to work in pairs or as partners throughout the course greatly enhances their progress.* This technique can be implemented early in the course through voluntary student selection, lottery, or other suitable methods. This system provides each student with a "partner" from whom to seek help and with whom to share ideas as together they proceed through the course.

Student Feedback

One of the most important ways to monitor your success as a teacher is student feedback. Sometimes it is necessary to create formal feedback vehicles rather than to rely upon impressions. In addition to Classroom Assessment Techniques (see below), techniques for obtaining feedback include:

- Giving sample questions that do not count toward the grade before testing and asking for the correct answer with a show of hands.
- Making certain there is open and ongoing communication.
- Asking students to write a letter to the next class describing the course.
- Having a post-mortem discussion with your class.

Classroom Assessment

Classroom Assessment Techniques (CATs) are based upon a series of teaching techniques to determine what students are learning. Results from CATs guide teachers in fine-tuning their teaching strategies to better meet student needs. They focus on evaluation of instruction and student involvement in the learning process. To be truly developmental, no credit should be granted for CAT activities. Some basic CATs that you can utilize in your classroom are summarized here.

The Minute Paper. At the end of class, ask students to give a written response on the *most important thing they learned and any questions they have concerning the day's topic.* The query can be worded in any manner—remember the response does not count toward the student's grade. If you are seeking a solution to a problem or an analysis of a situation, the question can be worded appropriately. Responses can then be used to start discussion for the next class session.

The Muddiest Point. Students are asked to identify *something about the topic that is confusing.* This question asks the students to identify where you have been unclear. They love this one. You can specify whether the students are to respond to the lecture, a demonstration, or other activity. Remember to specify the activity or you will get general answers of little value.

Defining Features Matrix. Prepare a handout with a matrix of three columns and several rows. At the top of the first two columns, list two distinct concepts that have potentially confusing similarities (e.g. hurricanes vs. tornados, Picasso vs. Matisse). In the third column, list the important characteristics of both concepts in no particular order. Give your students the handout and have them use the matrix to identify which characteristics belong to each of the two concepts. Collect their responses and *you will quickly find out which characteristics are giving your students the most trouble.*

What's the Principle? *This CAT is useful in courses requiring problem-solving.* After students figure out what type of problem they are dealing with, they often must decide what principle(s) to apply in order to solve the problem. This CAT provides students with a few problems and asks them to state the principle that best applies to each problem.

Classroom assessment resembles conducting classroom research more than most other pedagogical or andragogical techniques. CATS provide you with a continuous flow of information on student learning and quality of instruction in the classroom. These techniques are discussed in detail in *Classroom Assessment Techniques: A Handbook for College Teachers* (Angelo & Cross, 2009).

Finally, some of the most effective classroom strategies are creative and developed by the instructor. Too often teaching mainly consists of imitating the instructors we had during our own college careers. Such imitation limits the opportunity to try new and different teaching techniques. Research shows that student attention is improved when *activities in a classroom change every twenty minutes.* You should not feel obligated to stay with traditional classroom methods. If you feel like taking an innovative approach, share it with your students! They will usually be cooperative and appreciate that you are a risk taker and instructional innovator.

STUDENT CLASSROOM BEHAVIORS

Reports of problematic behaviors are on the rise nationally, not only in the classroom but in society at large (Kowalski, 2003). Some of these immature, irritating, or thoughtless behaviors or "classroom incivilities" include:

- lateness or leaving early
- inappropriate cellphone and laptop usage in class
- side conversations
- disregard for deadlines
- grade grubbing
- sniping remarks
- cheating

These behaviors are not just instructors' pet peeves. They have real costs including:

- distracting other students and instructor in class
- reducing student participation
- lowering other students' and instructor's motivation in or out of class
- affecting fairness in grading
- using instructor time unproductively
- feeling disrespected as a fellow learner or authority figure

Strategies

Based on these findings and a comprehensive literature review, Sorcinelli (2002) suggests four principles to reduce incivilities. The principles are broad enough that each one can be used to generate several concrete strategies:

& Techniques

1. Define expectations at the outset. Explicitly letting students know how you want them to behave in class avoids incivilities due to mismatched expectations.

2. Decrease anonymity. In classes large and small, students can sometimes engage in thoughtless behaviors because the atmosphere feels very depersonalized. Learn and use names consistently. Engage students one-on-one. Take advantage of office hours.

3. Seek feedback from students. Some student incivilities are due to perceived instructor incivilities – instructor's own lateness or disorganization, rudeness or interruptions when students are speaking. Seek feedback to double-check student perceptions of you.

4. Encourage active learning. Meaningful engagement has obvious benefits for student learning and performance, but it can also bring some side benefits with respect to student behavior in the classroom.

Certainly, teaching is a demanding activity. Most professionals can succeed with knowledge of the technical and intellectual content of their professions. A teacher, however, requires these competencies plus the ability to communicate with large numbers of individuals with divergent learning and behavior patterns. Here are some of the more common student behaviors in today's classrooms.

The Class Expert

The class expert has comments and knowledge concerning nearly any topic discussed in class. Be careful not to "put down" these students because it will discourage other students from contributing. Usually, an effective technique is to allow the expert to respond, then let peer pressure in the form of other student responses to eventually limit the expert's comments. If this approach does not solve the problem, an individual conference after the second or third class may be necessary. If all else fails, a verbal request for consideration of the other students during class would be in order. Prepared objectives, to which everyone's attention must be addressed, are a vital asset in curbing the class expert.

The Silent Class

Adjunct instructors commonly encounter silent classes because they are most likely to be teaching older and/or insecure students. Nonetheless, it is important that students be involved vocally in the class. Conversation and involvement are important to the learning process and provide feedback for the teacher. As stated earlier, the *first class can be important in breaking the silence barrier before it starts.* Some techniques to implement communication include: small group work, partnering, discussions of current events and personal experiences, brainstorming, icebreakers, and instructor anecdotes.

The Negative Student

Negative student behavior manifests itself in diverse ways. Sometimes students will challenge class discussion in a negative manner, or in other situations, they merely remain silent and appear to sulk for no apparent reason. It is important that you not allow the negative student syndrome to affect the class. The silent negative student usually will not greatly affect the class; however, the vocal negative student will. Initially, efforts should be made to involve the negative student in a positive or success-oriented question/answer format. Through this technique, you may be able to assess the interests of a negative student and stimulate participation. (Remember, the negative student made the effort to register for the course and to attend the class; thus he or she brings positive attributes.) An individual conference with the student often can clarify and help resolve the matter.

The Unruly Student

Although it is not commonplace, students occasionally surface even in the classroom. Inappropriate behavior can manifest itself in disagreements with other students (possibly physical), verbal outbursts, cursing, or general disruption. You should exhaust all reasonable strategies to control the situation, such as making eye contact with the student, politely asking for cooperation, or private consultation. If conditions reach the point where classroom order can no longer be maintained, ask the rest of the class to leave the room and then address the student with the problem directly in concert with procedures established by the institution.

MOTIVATION

One of the most widely accepted motivational theories is Maslow's hierarchy of needs, devised in the 1940s and updated in 2010 (Nauert). This hierarchy also applies to the learning process. The original hierarchy states that basic human needs fall into five categories. Although faculty cannot greatly affect the first of these needs, they can be effective in developing the final two.

To foster self-esteem in individuals creat a class environment based upon the "success" concept. Build the learning experience around student success and you create a productive learning/teaching situation.

Maslow's original pyramid of needs

Here are several strategies for developing a success-oriented classroom:

• Give students nonverbal encouragement.
• Provide students with positive reinforcement.
• Provide a structured situation in which students will feel comfortable.
• Emphasize that making mistakes is part of the learning proces.
• Establish realistic but challenging goals.

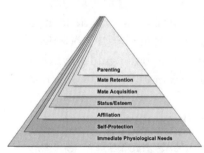

Revised pyramid of needs

Self-actualization occurs when a student's self-concept is developed. It is most easily realized through achievement and success. You can assist the student in achieving self-actualization in the following ways:

1. **Present some kind of challenge in each class**, but do not create insurmountable barriers.

2. **Treat your students as individuals.** Make every effort to prevent your class from becoming impersonal.

3. **Do not prejudge or stereotype students.** Don't label students or classes as "good" or "bad."

4. **Treat your students as adults.**

5. **Give consideration to students' personal problems.** Remember, adult students bring with them all the problems of life outside the classroom as well as those in your class.

6. **Provide a flexible classroom.** Rigid rules are considered demeaning by students. The flexible instructor is a more effective teacher. Being flexible does not imply the loss of authority. The teacher is always the authority in the classroom.

CLASSROOM TECHNIQUES

The First Class

It is normal when you face your first class to experience a certain amount of anxiety. Most teachers feel that this is a positive force that sharpens their skills. Here are some basic guidelines that will assist you in overcoming anxiety and in creating an effective and productive first meeting.

- Be over-prepared rather than under-prepared.

- Plan an activity that gets students involved immediately, such as an information-gathering exercise.

& Techniques

- Initiate casual conversation with and among students before going into the course specifics.

- Recount a personal anecdote or bring up a current news or college event to bridge the communication gap.

- Acknowledge students' confusion at the beginning of class. Confusion is not necessarily detrimental; it can be used to reduce student anxieties.

- Present the syllabus on an overhead and as a handout. Discuss it in detail with the class, emphasizing the sections describing student requirements.

- Conduct a full class. Teaching a full class creates the impression you're serious about the course.

- Be prepared with icebreakers, class-related questions with no specific answer, to stimulate discussion.

- Take care of housekeeping items such as office and restroom locations, if and when there are breaks, etc.

- Don't hesitate to share your background with the class. This shows you are as willing to share information as to gather it. But don't ask students for more about their backgrounds than you are willing to give about yours.

- Set the tone of the classroom by creating positive feelings about the course and your expectations for the class.

- Communicate to the class that you are a friendly, helpful person and not an inflexible disciplinarian.

- Don't fall into either of these two extremes in classroom behavior: the traditionally rigid "stay in your place" strategy and the laissez-faire "what shall we do today, gang" approach. Seek some happy medium.

The Lecture and Beyond

Since the 1990s, research on pedagogy has shifted from what instructors teach to what students learn. Thus, college leaders have turned a critical eye to the lecture itself. As a result, faculty are learning to make courses more active by seeding them with questions, ask-your-neighbor discussions and instant surveys. Keep in mind that active learning is hard work and student feedback reveals that interactive classes are more taxing than lectures. This is perhaps why, for all the talk of change, the lecture remains the dominant teaching method across a broad range of first- and second-year courses. However, integrating active learning strategies and opportunities into every course is a must and "letting go" of the lecture is always an option.

It is hard to let go of the idea that you are the best (and often only) source of information that the students have for your course. Where else will they get the information if not from you? Isn't it your job to give it to them? In reality, students have a variety of resources for every course they take: textbooks, Google, YouTube and other options exist in a range of formats to effectively meet the needs of the learner. Will they take advantage of those resources? A motivated student will learn about a topic whether you lecture on that topic or not (Adams and Gingras, 2018).

That being said, excellent lectures require more preparation than a good group activity or demonstration. Some of the requirements for preparing an effective lecture include:

- Carefully preparing notes, examples, formulae and facts, a main theme for the day and summary. Tell your students where you're going and when you get there.

- Making certain that the lecture is directed to the level of the students.

- Using anecdotes, concrete examples, and dramatic contrast to emphasize points.

- Using gestures and eye contact to keep communication channels open with the class.

& Techniques

- Using questions to stimulate and motivate students. Use questions to summarize at the conclusion of every major part of the lecture.

- Being conscious of your vocabulary. This is especially important for instructors in specialized areas where professional jargon and buzzwords may not be familiar to students.

- Intermixing active teaching activities and lecture techniques. Use a combination of traditional lecture, group work, problem solving and discussions.

- Taking advantage of all the teaching aids available, including audio/visual equipment, clickers and supplemental materials.

- Telling the students at the start what your intentions are and when you are changing topics.

- Summarizing—bring the lecture to a close with a summary review of major points or concepts. An effective summary includes repetition and reinforcement of the important points covered.

 It is important to *plan and develop proper lecture techniques*. Unfortunately lectures don't just happen, although it might be tempting to think they do.

Teaching experts note several characteristics of effective lectures:

- Students retain more of the material presented early in lectures, so make important points early and then expand upon them later.
- Lecture presentations are best supported with a variety of media.
- Require limited note-taking (provide students with copies of lecture notes or video lectures).
- A lecture no longer means that only the teacher talks. The best lectures include two-way communication that encourages active learning.

It is not appropriate to lecture when:

- Presenting complex, detailed or abstract information
- Dealing with information concerning feelings and attitudes
- Training in psychomotor (hands-on) skills
- Teaching high-level cognitive skills (e.g., synthesis and evaluation)

Question/Answer

The intelligent use of questions is probably the most effective teaching mechanism in existence. Proper questioning is the ultimate in good communication because it elicits critical thinking. There are several points to remember in questioning:

- **Ask an individual a specific question**, do not direct general questions to the entire class. After asking the question, pause and wait for the answer.
- **Use questions for all purposes**: to arouse curiosity, to assess the students' understanding of your presentation, to evaluate the comprehension of individuals, to allow students to provide input, and to digress from the class contribution.

& Techniques

- **Use questions creatively** whenever possible. A key question or an unusual question in each class session (even making a production of it) effectively stimulates classes and conveys information.
- **Use open-ended questions** to supplement lecture. These questions get students to comment or respond to the opening rather than give short answers. These types of questions would be: "What do you think of that?" or "How does that strike you?" Then call upon individual students by name. Avoid yes/no questions.

Discussion Strategies

Good discussion techniques have become a major part of good teaching. Discussions facilitate understanding as well as application and reinforcement. There are several points that should be remembered in developing a discussion plan:

- There must be an objective or purpose for the discussion; otherwise it will deteriorate into a meaningless gab session or an aimless sharing of opinions.

- A case study is an excellent vehicle for developing a meaningful discussion.

- A controversial issue is effective as long as students reach logical conclusions that can be expressed in writing.

- It is a good idea to involve students in the development of the discussion, including: planning the activities, monitoring the discussion, and presenting conclusions.

- Participation in discussion should count toward a student's final grade and should be clearly explained in the evaluation plan of the course so students know exactly the value of their contribution.

Some discussion strategies require intensive preparation time on the part of the instructor; others require less preparation time. The goals of a classroom discussion and not the time needed to prepare should govern which discussion strategies are utilized by the instructor:

1. **Chat Stations (high prep)**—Stations or posters are set up around the classroom, on the walls or on tables. Small groups of students go from station to station, performing some kind of task or responding to a prompt, either of which will result in a conversation.

2. **Values Continuum, Forced Debate (high prep)**—A statement that has two possible responses—agree or disagree—is read out loud. Depending on whether they agree or disagree with this statement, students move to one side of the room or the other. From that spot, students take turns defending their positions.

3. **Socratic Circles (high prep)**—Students read a text or group of texts and write discussion questions about the text. In class, students sit in a circle and an introductory, open-ended question is posed by the teacher or student discussion leader. From there, students continue the conversation, prompting one another to support their claims with textual evidence.

4. **Affinity Mapping (low prep)**—Students are given a broad question or problem that results in a variety of different ideas. Once lots of ideas have been generated, students group the ideas into similar categories, then label the categories and discuss why the ideas fit within them, how the categories relate to one another, and so on.

5. **Fishbowl (high prep)**—In this modified Socratic seminar, students take turns actively participating in the discussion and serving in the role of listeners. The inner circle consists of the active participants in the discussion. The outer circle consists of observers. All class members (whether in the inner or outer circle) are assigned a particular task such as the completion of a worksheet. The instructor does not participate and only interjects when necessary.

Student Panels

A student panel can be used as an alternative to lecturing by giving groups of students the opportunity to do the presenting. However, it must be structured so the specific objectives of the assignment are clearly defined prior to the panel presentation. Normally, a panel should consist of two to four members. Each member of the panel should be assigned specific topics or issues to be presented and/or defended. After the presentation, the rest of the class should be divided into discussion groups so these students can define their positions on the panel's topic. Instructors should remember to help students in developing open-ended questions for the rest of the class.

Learning Cells

In learning cells, students work in pairs to help each other learn; typically, the entire class is paired off for this activity. The pairs can work together in many different ways. It may involve a reading assignment in which the students share what they have read and then develop questions to present to one another. In this case they are demonstrating their reading comprehension and understanding of the issues while sharing their responses. Another possibility uses an open-question format where students can exercise their creativity in their responses or in a problem-solving situation. During the process the teacher moves about the room, going from pair to pair, seeking feedback and answering questions. Learning cells can be organized for an entire term or may be assigned for a single class meeting.

Buzz Groups

As an in-class activity, the buzz group's purpose is to solve a specific problem or compare and contrast an issue. The instructor identifies the discussion topic or problem and allows students to form small groups, usually of three to five students. The students develop their own discussion guidelines for reaching a solution to the issue. The solution is prepared for presentation, possibly on a flip chart or overhead transparency for the following class session. Occasionally the instructor may have a solution prepared and use it as a discussion of the differences between the student buzz groups' and the instructor's conclusions. Buzz groups should not be confused with small group projects.

Buzz groups can be used as a quick conclusion activity that takes only 10 to 15 minutes of class time.

Out-of-Class Activities

Some Quick Do's and Don'ts

1. Provide detail in your assignment description. Research has shown that students frequently prefer some guiding constraints when completing assignments (Bean, 1996), and that more detail (within reason) can lead to more successful student responses.

2. Use open-ended questions. The most effective and challenging assignments focus on questions that lead students to thinking and explaining (Gardner, 2011).

3. Provide models–both successful and unsuccessful models (Miller, 2007). These models could be provided by past students, or models you have created yourself.

4. Include a way for students to make the assignment their own. In their study, Hass and Osborn (2007) confirmed the importance of personal engagement for students when completing an assignment.

5. Do not ask too many questions in your assignment. In an effort to challenge students, instructors often err in the other direction, asking more questions than students can reasonably address in a single assignment without losing focus.

6. Do not expect or suggest that there is an "ideal" response to the assignment.

7. Do not provide vague or confusing commands. Do students know what you mean when they are asked to "examine" or "discuss" a topic?

Just in Time Teaching (JiTT)

Just-in-Time Teaching is a teaching and learning strategy based on the interaction between web-based study assignments and an active learner classroom. Students respond electronically to carefully constructed web-based assignments which are due shortly before class. The instructor reads the student submissions "just-in-time" and shapes the classroom lesson to meet the students' needs. The heart of JiTT is the "feedback loop" formed by the students' out-of-class preparation that shapes what happens during the in-class time with the instructor.

Although Just-in-Time Teaching makes heavy use of the web, it is not to be confused with either distance learning (DL) or with computer-aided instruction (CAI). Virtually all JiTT instruction occurs in a classroom with instructors. The web materials act primarily as a communication tool, an added as a pedagogical resource, and secondarily as content provider and organizer. JiTT is also not a tool to "process" large numbers of students by using computers to do grading.

The JiTT web component is comprised of WarmUps and Puzzles. These are short, web-based assignments that encourage students to think about the upcoming lesson and answer a few simple questions prior to class. These questions, when fully discussed, often have complex answers. The students are expected to develop the answers as far as they can on their own. The job is completed in the classroom. These assignments are due just a few hours before class time and the responses are delivered to the instructor electronically to form the framework for the in-class activities that follow.

JiTT fosters feelings of ownership among students since the interactive lessons are based on their own wording and understanding of the relevant course material and issues.

Projects

Student projects are one way students can learn outside the classroom. Projects may consist of in-depth research into a class topic or a community-based activity such as agency visitations, interviews, or case studies. A properly developed project should allow students to choose from a variety of related activities within their own sphere of interest. After topics are selected, instructor expectations for completion of the project should be clarified.

Case Studies

Case studies are have long been used in business schools, law schools, medical schools and the social sciences, but *they can be used in any discipline when instructors want students to explore how what they have learned applies to real world situations.* Case studies actively engage students in figuring out the principles by abstracting from the examples. Students develop skills in:

- Problem solving
- Analytical tools, quantitative and/or qualitative, depending on the case
- Decision making in complex situations
- Coping with ambiguities

In a good case study, the instructor establishes the scenario, the objectives of the case, and the problem(s) that may be encountered. Students may then be given time to read and research the project and write their case paper or make an oral presentation which can lead to student discussions that reach consensus or a conclusion. Case studies are normally assigned to individual students and not to groups. Asking students to role-play the part of the people involved in the case is an innovative approach to case analysis.

Field Trips

Field trips should be planned so that the entire session of the field trip is on location. The class activities and trip objectives should be outlined prior to the trip. Arrange the class in small groups and specify to the students what they are to observe. At the conclusion of the visit, meet to discuss the major points observed and any conclusions to be made. The most effective field trips include credit toward the grade and require a written or oral report, including, perhaps a field trip reflection Minute Paper or worksheet.

INSTRUCTIONAL AIDS

Recent studies demonstrate that student retention of information improves markedly when faculty make use of appropriate instructional aids. Technology has opened a new vista of tools for use in the classroom. In addition, there are also some tried and true instructional aids available to you. A few examples are listed below. Some of the guidelines governing the use of such aids include making certain that *instructional aids support the lesson objective, build on previous learning, appeal to students and maintain student attention, contain quality graphs, text and photos as required and encourage student participation when appropriate.*

Computers/Multimedia

Integrating interactive multimedia and tools, including smartphones, can make teaching more efficient, effective, powerful and flexible. Multimedia tools provide students with individualized activities that accommodate differences in students' levels of preparation and learning. To begin, transform your course notes into electronic files (PDFs), find royalty-free, high-quality illustrations online, do real-time calculations and processing, engage students in interactive collaborations and bring text, graphics, animation, sound and video into the classroom.

Multimedia Use PROS
- Advance prep results in more effective student learning.
- Allows effective presentation of complex concepts, data and other information.
- Encourages student attention.

Computer/ Multimedia Use CONS
- Requires expertise, familiarity and software.
- May create a distance between you and your students if there is no student interaction.
- Can result in hardware, app or software problems.

Video/Screencasting

Having videos uploaded onto video sharing sites such as You-Tube, Dropbox or Vimeo allows students easy access. In class, the capability to easily stop, freeze, zoom, and replay is particularly helpful for both instructors and students. Out of class, video lectures and screencasts may be watched by students at their convenience. Common examples of screencasts are onscreen tutorials, video lessons, or slideshare presentations. The viewer absorbs the screencast information at her/his own pace. *QuickTime for Mac offers a simple screen recording feature to record screencasts. Microsft Expression Encoder is an advanced audio/video encoding application that does screen recording in its free version. Google Hangout is a free cloud-based screencasting tool.*

The possibilities for expanded video use are nearly endless. Your college's instructional support department and its library have equipment and can offer support for instructors who wish to develop their own video lectures and clips. Videos are not only attention getters, but provide the opportunity for direct student involvement when students produce their own videos. However, *instructors must indicate to the students the learning objectives behind any videos and combine the video with discussion, a written report, or other activity.*

Electronic Options for Collecting Observations/Answers

When using videos, you can ask students to submit observations and answers in real time using Twitter and other social-networking tools.

Give students a prompt prior to starting the video clip and then have them live-tweet their responses during the video with a hashtag and your class number. Socrative and Poll Everywhere provide more privacy than Twitter. Instructors can use either site to collect students' responses via computers, tablets, or text messages.

Interactive Whiteboards (IWB)

The IWB is a touch-sensitive display that connects to a computer and a projector. It is both an output and input device. You can see all images as you would on a computer screen. You can write on it with electronic pens and use your finger as a mouse. Use of whiteboards is not limited to technology faculty. Users may be found across the entire spectrum of academic disciplines, including math and health sciences. Use of the board in mathematics instruction is particularly popular. Complex formulas can be reused or refreshed without having to be rewritten, and notes created during class can be printed out immediately to be distributed and shared with students. According to a 2009 study published in *EDUCAUSE Review Online*, 42 percent of college faculty surveyed reported that they would like to use electronic whiteboards in the classroom, but needed additional help with the technology.

IWB technology adds value for students who are already immersed in the world of media and expect visual stimulation. However, as Quashie (2009) concluded, their interactive features may not be appropriate for every lesson, and it is possible to use IWBs without any interactivity. However, under the right conditions, they can help promote student engagement and foster content area learning in a learner-centered classroom (Curwood, 2009).

Flipcharts

When used in the classroom, the flipchart has many advantages over a chalkboard or projector. It is especially useful for small groups to record their discussions and conclusions. Instructors can record major points of a presentation and have room to add notes, descriptions, or comments. A flipchart and felt-tip pen can be one of the most effective tools in the active classroom.

Handouts

Is the use of print media in the classroom passé? No. Photographs, reproductions of paintings, drawings, murals, cartoons, and other print materials are invaluable supplemental aids. Many of these items are suitable for long-term use. Although sometimes overused or viewed as outdated, handouts are still a valuable instrument for instructors. PDF and other document production software make preparing and updating easy. Handouts should be used for material that students will need for reference, such as important definitions, computations, or position statements for discussion. A serious note of caution: be careful of copyright violations! Your supervisor or department head should be able to provide you with the Fair Use guidelines you will need to follow.

 NOTE: When planning to use an instructional aid, be sure you have all the equipment you require before the class begins, whether it's chalk, markers, flipchart easels or the projector.

INTEGRATING TECHNOLOGY

An effective teacher is an excellent communicator who improves his or her presentation skills. One of the most important aspects of communicating is shaping both content and style to fit your audience. In the classroom, if you cannot communicate in a way that is both comprehensible and interesting to your students, their learning will be greatly reduced (McKeachie 2014).

Much has been made about the generation of technology-savvy students currently in and entering college. It has been suggested these "digital natives" Prensky (2001) possess unprecedented levels of skill with information technology and that they think about and use technology very differently from earlier student cohorts.

A paper published in June 2017 *Teaching and Teacher Education* reaches the opposite conclusion. The digital native is a myth, the paper's authors claim: a yeti with a smartphone (Kirschner and Bruyckere). Digital natives are assumed to be able to multi-task, but the evidence for this is scant. Texting during university lectures almost certainly comes at a cognitive cost.

According to a 2017 EDUCAUSE study, a student's major was an important predictor of preferences for technology in the classroom with engineering students having the highest preference for technology in the classroom (67.8 percent), followed by business students (64.3 percent). *That same study concluded that* *the majority of students prefer classes with moderate use of technology. This preference has remained unchanged.*

& Techniques

Presentation Software

Presentation software, as the name suggests, presents classroom material in a format similar to an overhead projector, saves the presentation, and allows changes that reflect student participation or new information. One of the most popular types of presentation software is PowerPoint™ published by Microsoft. PowerPoint™ is here to stay. However, there are now many free PowerPoint™ alternatives. These include Google Slides, Prezi Basic, SlideDog, Slides and Slides.

Presentation software as a teaching aid improves instruction by:
- building a knowledge base for class discussion or as reinforcement of your presentation,
- increasing the comprehension level of key concepts,
- analyzing complex material through data utilization, and assessing instructional quality through summary.

Tips for Perfecting PowerPoint Lectures:
- Use the 6-8 rule: 6-8 words per line and 6-8 lines per screen.
- Don't write everything you want to say on your slides. You are the primary source of information and the presentation is secondary.
- Use 28 to 40 point font sizes.
- Use sans serif fonts (e.g., Arial) rather than serif fonts (e.g., Times New Roman).
- Avoid underlined and *italicized* words, when possible.
- High contrast colors work best (e.g., white and black or yellow and blue).
- Use slide effects sparingly because they can be distracting.
- Test run each presentation. Twice.
- Focus on the information, not on the technology.

Internet

Finding information online is second nature to all students. Making good use of the results returned by a search engine requires fundamental research skills as well as the skills to judge credible from unreliable sources. Search engines allow you and your students to locate vast amounts of material valuable to your class. Teaching students to filter and evaluate that material is one of the instructor's most important lessons. Start by recommending reliable websites and sources acceptable for student use. Make sure students understand proper use of citation when integrating materials found online into written assignments and other projects. Asking students to analyze and synthesize information found online is one strategy to reduce plagiarism (whether intentional or unintentional).

Course Websites

About half of all faculty create course websites or use their colleges' online Learning Management Systems (LMS) to provide more detailed course information. There are public-facing class websites which, as the name implies, means that all course materials posted to the site are public. If you don't want your course material to be available to the public, a Canvas or Blackboard site is normally restricted to your students. *For a public-facing course website, WordPress is an excellent platform.* WordPress is used widely and so extensive help is available online. The platform allows easy integration of visual media, WordPress pages may be used for static content (syllabus, course description) and posts are dated (perfect for lectures, tips, announcements). WordPress is mobile friendly and WordPress sites are easily customized.

All faculty websites, regardless of the chosen platform, should include audio and video materials, as well as downloadable files. Keep in mind, however, that a course website must be kept up to date, but once designed and launched course websites can be invaluable tools. Your department or college IT support may provide templates.

& Techniques

Social Media

Young adults have consistently been the heaviest users of social media by a substantial margin, and today that's even more true: a staggering 90 percent of them use social media, according to a 2015 Pew Research Center study. That's a 78 percent increase from the 12 percent who were using social media back in 2005. Incorporating social media into the lesson plan is an additional way for students to understand the material they're already studying. As of 2013, 41 percent of 8,000 faculty surveyed said they used social media in the classroom. This use continues to experience steady year-to-year growth. Regardless of how social media is used, faculty should keep in mind issues relating to privacy—their own as well as that of their students.

 Evidence suggests that many students are not comfortable with their teachers accessing their personal sites. Of college students surveyed by Strader, Reed, Suh, and Njoroge (2016), one-third expressed concerns about privacy and identity management. Students indicated they did not want faculty to view their profiles on Facebook, concerned that the content on their profiles could influence their grades or treatment and interactions in the classroom. For faculty who wish to use social media in the classroom, always separate personal and professional social media accounts. Make social media an optional part of the course.

Email

According to a 2017 study, "Digital Faculty: Professors, Teaching and Technology": "A majority of faculty report that they respond to at least 90 percent of all student emails with 24 hours." Every college or university has email capability. Establish an email address as soon as possible. A word of caution, however: manage your teaching email by establishing a unique address available to all students (separate from the address to which your non-teaching email goes).

A simple email application to help communicate with students is establishing a listserv for your class. *A listserv allows you and anyone in your class to communicate with the entire class simultaneously by posting a single email message.*

PLANNING

In teaching, experts and practitioners universally agree that one element ranks highest in importance: planning. Adequate planning is essential to reaching the desired learning outcomes. Teachers who practice "off-the-cuff" teaching are doomed to fail. Although there are many planning support mechanisms, all are essentially built upon one premise—to adequately outline the class step-by- step. Prior to embarking upon the planning process, however, it is important to develop specific objectives for the course. *Properly stated objectives not only provide guidelines for both the teacher and the student throughout the course, they prevent students from deviating from course content.*

There are structured methods for the development of a proper course plan. The simplest method begins with the catalog description of the course you are teaching. This should help you decide upon the broad goals for the course. Then under each goal you can list your objectives. Properly written objectives will use such descriptors as

First Time Teacher Revelation #27

"The mediocre teacher tells. The good teacher explains. The superior teacher demonstrates. The great teacher inspires."

—William Arthur Ward

write, solve, contrast, compare, describe, identify, and list. Do not use general descriptors such as enjoy, appreciate, discuss, believe, and grasp because there is no way to evaluate them.

Most courses can be adequately covered in eight to twelve objectives. Writing too many objectives leads to a lack of clear direction in the course.

There are three major components to creating a formal teaching plan: the course outline, the lesson plan and the course syllabus.

> **1.** The lesson plan is the instrument the instructor uses day-to-day. **2.** The course outline is the instructor's guideline to course content. **3.** The syllabus is to some degree a combination of the two.

Course Outline

Whereas the lesson plan is a daily map for teachers to ensure their direction in a given session, the course outline is much more comprehensive and allows you to monitor the flow of the entire course. The outline normally is created from the course objectives. An outline format is usually used with no greater detail than a list of objectives with two or three subtopics under each.

When developing an outline, you must determine whether the course needs to be structured in a chronological or topical format. *A chronological format requires that fundamentals be mastered before moving on to more advanced concepts, whereas a topical outline can be modified and rearranged with much more flexibility, because there is no concern that students have prior knowledge.*

Lesson Plan

The format for the lesson varies depending upon the instructor and the type of course being taught. The only thing universally agreed upon is that the lesson plan should be written down. Each plan should list a definite purpose that gives the main points of the lesson, and each should be numbered and arranged as part of the total plan for the course. For example, references, research, and quotes may be part of the formal lesson plan, while anecdotal comments may be written in as marginal notes, and outside references such as newspaper clippings handled as unique entities. Ask yourself the question that students often ask—What are we going to do today and why are we going to do it?

A lesson plan is made up of a number of parts
They are:

- A list of definitions for explanation
- The objectives of the class
- The impact or purpose of the class
- A definite plan for instructor activities
- The outline of student activities
- The assignment for the next session

Below is a lesson plan model you can use in preparing for classes.

LESSON PLAN

Course number and name _____

Date_____

Session # _____

Topic(s) to be covered _____

_____

Instructional aids, materials_____

Definitions to be covered _____

_____

Class objective(s) _____

_____

Student activities or exercises _____

_____

Instructor activities _____

_____

Major impact or thought _____

Assignment _____

_____

& Techniques

The lesson plans for a course should be accumulated and kept chronologically in a permanent file or notebook to eliminate the need to develop a completely new lesson plan each time you teach the same course. Maintained in chronological order, they are available for easy reference and for review and update as each new class begins. Reviewing your lesson plans eliminates dated and irrelevant material.

Syllabus

A syllabus is defined as "a concise statement of the main points of a course of study or subject" and is considered the official document for the course. It should be shared with students and may even be a permanent part of the college's instructional archives. It could become a legal document in case of litigation.

Despite universal recognition of the syllabus's importance in course preparation and instruction, no single format has wide acceptance. While there is wide variation in the content of the syllabus, most faculty agree that a syllabus should contain these main parts:

1. The **complete name of the course**, including the course number and section.

2. **Course description**. A narrative description of the course based upon the college catalog description.

3. The **faculty member's name** and preferred title.

4. The **faculty member's availability**. This should include: office hours, meeting location, phone, and email address. Include procedures for arranging an appointment since most adjunct faculty do not have individual offices.

5. The **required materials**. This should include the text(s), outside readings and manuals, reference materials, supplies, and web page addresses, if applicable.

6. Any **course requirements and prerequisites**.

7. The **course objectives**. Be specific. Clarify and articulate the objectives that the students will achieve by the end of the course. Number them for emphasis.

8. The **specific assignments**, projects, etc., to be completed by the students.

9. A **complete listing of outside resources**, readings, and group activities, etc.

10. **Attendance policy**. Clarify expectations concerning tardiness and quiz/test makeups.

11. **Classroom regulations**. This should include academic honesty, behavior expectations, harassment and general operational procedures.

12. **Evaluation plan and grading standards**. Specify the weighting of all graded assignments: tests, quizzes, class participation, projects, group work evaluation, and field trips, etc.

13. **Emergency procedures**. Include emergency phones, evacuation procedures, medical assistance, and campus security.

The syllabus should be distributed to the students on the first day of class. Time should be taken to discuss the details of the syllabus. In fact, it is good practice to go over the syllabus during the second meeting of the class. *Describe in detail the student activities and how* *they relate to certain assignments and objectives. Remember that a syllabus is an essential part of any course and it should be shown that respect in its development and use.*

Evaluation Plan & Charting

An evaluation plan that is understood by all students is necessary for the proper assignment of grades. The evaluation plan is a simple chart that contains all of the factors used in the assignment of grades. The simplest and most easily understood plan is one that assigns points for each element graded. This is easy to understand and requires only simple arithmetic to arrive at an accurate grade assignment. A sample chart is shown below:

EVALUATION CHART			
Grade Factors	Percent of Final Grade	Possible Points	Points Received
Test #1	15	30	26
Test #2	15	30	28
Test #3	30	60	54
Outside Project	10	20	15
Class Participation	10	20	16
Group work	10	20	20
Paper	10	20	20
Total	**100**	**200**	**179**

Note that the grade factors are listed in the first column. In the second column, the percent to be assigned to the final grade is shown. It should always add up to 100. The third column indicates the total number of points possible for each activity. These values are determined by multiplying the total number of points for the course (200) times the assigned percentage. This provides the "weighting" for the different grade factors. Here the total need not add up to 100 but each must reflect the percentages of column 2. Note in the sample evaluation the student earned 179 points of a possible 200. The percentage grade then can easily be obtained by dividing 179 (points earned) by 200 (points possible) or 89.5 percent. Obviously, this simple chart can easily be placed on a computer program for rapid and accurate calculation.

TESTING AND GRADING

The assignment of grades is one of the most important and difficult tasks in teaching. Regardless of the process adopted, it is difficult to eliminate all subjectivity from assigning grades. Thus it is important that the instructor develop the best evaluation and grading skills possible. Modern technology has improved the process, at least for multiple-choice questions, by providing test validity through item analysis techniques.

 Establishing the criteria for grades and sharing it with students as part of the course syllabus starts the evaluation process very early in the course.

The major types of tests used in college classes are: essay, multiple choice and recall. In special circumstances, performance, oral and short-answer tests may also be utilized.

Essay Tests/Questions

Essay tests work at any level of the learning hierarchy by incorporating analysis and synthesis. Although essay tests require considerable time for students, they give significant insight into what the students are learning and what they are hearing in the classroom.

There are several factors to remember when writing test questions that require essay answers:

- Questions should be related to course objectives.

- Questions should incorporate a significant content.

- Questions should be worded so excessive time is not spent on trivial matters.

- The student must have sufficient background to respond adequately to the question.

- Questions should not be ambiguous or deceptive.

- Questions should not ask for student opinions.

& Techniques

Essay questions, if constructed and graded properly, are the most accurate of the possible testing techniques. Grading essay questions also presents the greatest challenge and *the best way to judge an essay response is for you to write your response, listing important comments by priority. Assigning points to these prioritized criteria will give a degree of grading objectivity.*

Multiple-Choice Tests/Questions

Large classes and computerized scoring make multiple-choice tests the most used tests today. In fact, computer programs exist which allow the instructor to change multiple-choice tests for different classes of the same course. This is accomplished by developing a large database of questions and randomly selecting from the database.

The actual construction of the multiple-choice tests has several general guidelines. They include:

- Do not include answers that are obviously correct or incorrect, including impossible responses or distracters.

- Be sure the correct answers are scattered throughout the response mechanism.

- Provide four possible responses to minimize the guess factor.

- Do not use "all of the above" or "none of the above."

- Do not use the terms never, always or likely since they may divert the student.

- Do not include "trick" or misleading questions or overly difficult vocabulary.

- Present multiple-choice questions positively rather than negatively.

- Be consistent with the format to avoid confusion.

- Keep choices approximately the same length since incorrect answers are frequently shorter than correct ones.

Multiple-choice tests measure discrimination abilities as well as simple knowledge and should always deal with a significant aspect of the course.

Recall and Completion Tests/Questions

The compromise between the multiple-choice test and the essay test is the short answer or recall test. Short-answer questions can be written on a specific topic or point and do not require as much time and effort as essay questions, while allowing for the creativity and analysis not permissible with multiple-choice questions.
Some suggestions for developing recall questions are:

- Give information concerning the answer prior to the answer blank.

- Qualify information so students are clear about the response.

- Include responses at the analysis and synthesis level.

- Pose questions with only one correct response.

- Allow sufficient space for the response.

- Avoid patterns of responses.

- Avoid direct quotes.

- Avoid specific descriptors or adjectives.

 The short answer and recall tests allow the student to present the solution to a problem or to develop a hypothesis. Such questions may allow students to compare the differences between two statements, items, or activities not possible in the use of all other questions save the essay.

True/False Tests/Questions

True/false questions are not commonly used at the college level any longer. Although they may have their place in sampling student responses to a learning activity, they generally are not accepted as objective or valid in testing situations.

Regardless of the types of tests used, there are several criteria that must be kept in mind in assigning grades.

- **Communicate the criteria for grades** at the beginning of the course and clarify any misunderstandings then.
- **Include criteria other than test scores** such as class participation, projects, and research.
- **Avoid irrelevant factors** such as tardiness and unexcused absences.
- **Weigh grading criteria carefully**—do not give equal credit for activities that are obviously not equal.
- **Grade students by their individual achievement**, not other students—the "bell curve" standard was abandoned years ago.

FACULTY SELF-EVALUATION

Any dynamic process like teaching is of little value unless it can be assessed to determine if it is achieving its goals. After instructors feel they have adequately planned, expending hours of time and energy, they will want some indication of the fruits of that planning. One method that can be used to evaluate your teaching technique and course structure is with a faculty self-evaluation.

Although most colleges have official faculty evaluation forms that they either require or recommend using, faculty may wish to develop a self-evaluation form. A few underlying principles for self-evaluations include:

- The form should not be so long that students eventually check anything to complete the form.

- It should be logically organized into classroom, course, and instructor evaluation.

- The evaluation code should be easily understood. Avoid excessive numbering, such as 1-10. Students easily understand a simple grading system (A-E).

- It should, of course, be anonymous and should be given prior to the class session during which the final examination is held.

- The students should be informed that only constructive criticism and/or reinforcement is of value.

A suggested faculty self-evaluation form is shown on the page opposite. These are only some of the questions that can be asked and their statistical validity has not been tested. However, it provides suggested guidelines for the development of an instrument for your use.

Even though students are often biased, the value of student input is unquestionable. Most students will respond honestly and sincerely and, over the course of several classes, the statistically deviant responses can be identified and disregarded.

FACULTY EVALUATION FORM

CLASS:_____

DATE: _____

INSTRUCTIONS: Please grade each factor on a scale of A-E in terms of your perception of the teacher's behavior or characteristics.

CLASSROOM EVALUATION

Preparation for class   _____

Communication of classroom expectation   _____

Command of subject matter   _____

Professionalism of classroom behavior   _____

Match of tests and evaluations to course objectives   _____

Encouragement of student participation   _____

Clarity and conciseness of assignments   _____

COURSE-RELATED FACTORS

Course objectives clearly defined   _____

Course content clearly reflects catalog description   _____

Appropriateness of project assignments   _____

Value of field trips   _____

Appropriateness of topic selection for outside assignments _____

Use supplemental teaching aids, support
materials and other props   _____

INSTRUCTOR EVALUATION

Consideration for differing opinions   _____

Consideration for individuals as persons   _____

Willingness to give individual help   _____

Utilized technology and instructional aids   _____

Organized presentation   _____

Instructor's greatest strengths: _____

Instructor's greatest weaknesses: _____

Suggestions to improve course: _____

_____

COPYRIGHT FAIR USE GUIDELINES FOR COLLEGE FACULTY

Courtesy of the Stanford Copyright and Fair Use Center, Stanford University Libraries, Stanford University, 2017 (http://fairuse.stanford.edu/).

What Types of Creative Work Does Copyright Protect?

Copyright protects works such as poetry, movies, CD-ROMs, video games, videos, plays, paintings, sheet music, recorded music performances, novels, software code, sculptures, photographs, choreography and architectural designs.

To qualify for copyright protection, a work must be "fixed in a tangible medium of expression." This means that the work must exist in some physical form for at least some period of time, no matter how brief. Virtually any form of expression will qualify as a tangible medium, including a computer's random access memory (RAM), the recording media that capture all radio and television broadcasts, and the scribbled notes on the back of an envelope that contain the basis for an impromptu speech.

In addition, the work must be original — that is, independently created by the author. It doesn't matter if an author's creation is similar to existing works, or even if it is arguably lacking in quality, ingenuity or aesthetic merit. So long as the author toils without copying from someone else, the results are protected by copyright.

Permission: What Is It and Why Do I Need It?

Obtaining copyright permission is the process of getting consent from a copyright owner to use the owner's creative material. Obtaining permission is often called "licensing"; when you have permission, you have a license to use the work. Permission is often (but not always) required because of intellectual property laws that protect creative works such as text, artwork, or music. (These laws are

& Techniques

explained in more detail in the next section.) If you use a copyrighted work without the appropriate permission, you may be violating—or "infringing"—the owner's rights to that work. Infringing someone else's copyright may subject you to legal action. As if going to court weren't bad enough, you could be forced to stop using the work or pay money damages to the copyright owner.

As noted above, permission is not always required. In some situations, you can reproduce a photograph, a song, or text without a license. Generally, this will be true if the work has fallen into the public domain, or if your use qualifies as what's called a "fair use." Both of these legal concepts involve quite specific rules. In most cases, however, permission is required, so it is important to never assume that it is okay to use a work without permission.

Many people operate illegally, either intentionally or through ignorance. They use other people's work and never seek consent. This may work well for those who fly under the radar—that is, if copyright owners never learn of the use, or don't care enough to take action.

Obtaining Clearance for Coursepacks

It is the instructor's obligation to obtain clearance for materials used in class. Instructors typically delegate this task to one of the following:

- Clearance services. These services are the easiest method of clearance and assembly.
- University bookstores or copy shops. University policies may require that the instructor delegate the task to the campus bookstore, copy shop, or to a special division of the university that specializes in clearances.

Using a Clearance Service

It can be time-consuming to seek and obtain permission for the 20, 30, or more articles you want to use in a coursepack. Fortunately, private clearance services will, for a fee, acquire permission and assemble coursepacks on your behalf. After the coursepacks are created and sold, the clearance service collects royalties and distributes the payments to the rights holders. Educational institutions may require that the instructor use a specific clearance service.

The largest copyright clearing service is the Copyright Clearance Center (www.copyright.com), which clears millions of works from thousands of publishers and authors.

In 2001, XanEdu (www.xanedu.com), acquired the coursepack service formerly known as Campus Custom Publishing. In addition to providing traditional coursepack assembly, XanEdu offers an electronic online service that provides supplemental college course materials directly to the instructor's desktop via the internet.

Educational Uses of Non-Coursepack Materials

Unlike academic coursepacks, other copyrighted materials can be used without permission in certain educational circumstances under copyright law or as a fair use. "Fair use" is the right to use portions of copyrighted materials without permission for purposes of education, commentary or parody.

The Code of Best Practices in Fair Use for Media Literacy Education

In 2008, the Center for Media and Social Impact, in connection with American University, unveiled a guide of fair use practices for instructors in K–12 education, in higher education, in nonprofit organizations that offer programs for children and youth, and in adult education. The guide identifies five principles that represent acceptable practices for the fair use of copyrighted materials. You can learn more at the center's website, (www.cmsimpact.org).

Guidelines Establish a Minimum, Not a Maximum

In a case alleging 75 instances of infringement in an educational setting, 70 instances were not infringing because of fair use and for other reasons. The infringements were alleged because of the posting of copyrighted books within a university's e-reserve system. The court viewed the Copyright Office's 1976 Guidelines for Educational Fair Use as a minimum, not a maximum standard. The court then proposed its own fair use standard—10% of a book with less than ten chapters, or of a book that is not divided into chapters, or no more than one chapter or its equivalent in a book of more than ten chapters.—*Cambridge University Press v. Georgia State University*, Case 1:08-cv-01425-OD (N.D. Ga., May 11, 2012).

What is the Difference Between the Guidelines and Fair Use Principles?

The educational guidelines are similar to a treaty that has been adopted by copyright owners and academics. Under this arrangement, copyright owners will permit uses that are outlined in the guidelines. In other fair use situations, the only way to prove that a use is permitted is to submit the matter to court or arbitration. In other words, in order to avoid lawsuits, the various parties have agreed on what is permissible for educational uses, codified in these guidelines.

What is an "Educational Use?"

The educational fair use guidelines apply to material used in educational institutions and for educational purposes. Examples of "educational institutions" include K-12 schools, colleges, and universities. Libraries, museums, hospitals, and other nonprofit institutions also are considered educational institutions under most educational fair use guidelines when they engage in nonprofit instructional, research, or scholarly activities for educational purposes.

"Educational Purposes" are:

- noncommercial instruction or curriculum-based teaching by educators to students at nonprofit educational institutions
- planned noncommercial study or investigation directed toward making a contribution to a field of knowledge, or
- presentation of research findings at noncommercial peer conferences, workshops, or seminars.

Rules for Reproducing Text Materials for Use in Class

The guidelines permit a teacher to make one copy of any of the following: a chapter from a book; an article from a periodical or newspaper; a short story, short essay, or short poem; a chart, graph, diagram, drawing, cartoon, or picture from a book, periodical, or newspaper.

Teachers may not photocopy workbooks, texts, standardized tests, or other materials that were created for educational use. The guidelines were not intended to allow teachers to usurp the profits of educational publishers. In other words, educational publishers do not consider it a fair use if the copying provides replacements or substitutes for the purchase of books, reprints, periodicals, tests, workbooks, anthologies, compilations, or collective works.

Rules for Reproducing Music

A music instructor can make copies of excerpts of sheet music or other printed works, provided that the excerpts do not constitute a "performable unit," such as a whole song, section, movement, or aria. In no case can more than 10% of the whole work be copied and the number of copies may not exceed one copy per pupil. Printed copies that have been purchased may be edited or simplified provided that the fundamental character of the work is not distorted or the lyrics altered.

A student may make a single recording of a performance of copyrighted music for evaluation or rehearsal purposes, and the educational institution or individual teacher may keep a copy. In addition, a single copy of a sound recording owned by an educational institution or an individual teacher (such as a tape, disc, or cassette) of copyrighted music may be made for the purpose of constructing aural exercises or examinations, and the educational institution or individual teacher can keep a copy.

Rules for Recording and Showing Television Programs

Nonprofit educational institutions can record television programs transmitted by network television and cable stations. The institution can keep the tape for 45 days, but can only use it for instructional purposes during the first ten of the 45 days. After the first ten days, the video recording can only be used for teacher evaluation purposes, to determine whether or not to include the broadcast program in the teaching curriculum. If the teacher wants to keep it within the curriculum, he or she must obtain permission from the copyright owner. The recording may be played once by each individual teacher in the course of related teaching activities in classrooms and similar places devoted to instruction (including formalized home instruction). The recorded program can be repeated once if necessary, although there are no standards for determining what is and is not necessary. After 45 days, the recording must be erased or destroyed.

A video recording of a broadcast can be made only at the request of and only used by individual teachers. A television show may not be regularly recorded in anticipation of requests—for example, a teacher cannot make a standing request to record each episode of a PBS series. Only enough copies may be reproduced from each recording to meet the needs of teachers, and the recordings may not be combined to create teaching compilations. All copies of a recording must include the copyright notice on the broadcast program as recorded and (as mentioned above) must be erased or destroyed after 45 days.

CONCLUSION

Teaching college part-time can be an incredibly rewarding activity. You increase your own knowledge of the course material and you gain new skills in presenting and communicating that could very well improve your skills at work.

You need to take your task as teacher as seriously as you take the other important parts of your life. You are as much responsible for your students learning the material as they are. You are directly responsible for your students' success.

By planning, planning, and overplanning, you can feel confident in your abilities to cover the course objectives and to grade your students fairly and without bias. In addition, if you are unsure about any of your planning instruments, remember that there are others around you who want you to succeed. Show your plans to your supervisor, coordinator, or a teacher whom you respect.

Getting to know your students and the experiences they bring to your class will give you considerable appreciation for the diversity of your community. Using active learning techniques will bring out these experiences and give all your students the confidence they will need to compete in today's job market.

Now, go teach and don't forget to have enough confidence to have fun!

REFERENCES

Adams, P., & Gingras, H. (2018). Blended Learning and Flipped Classrooms: A Comprehensive Guide. Ann Arbor: The Part-Time Press.

Angelo, T. A., & Cross, P. K. (2009). Classroom Assessment Techniques: A Handbook for College Teachers, 2nd ed. San Francisco: Jossey-Bass.

Babson Survey Research Group (2012). "Digital Faculty: Professors and Technology, 2012."

Bean, J.C. (1996). Engaging ideas: The professor's guide to integrating writing, critical thinking, and active learning in the classroom. San Francisco: Jossey-Bass.

Curwood, J. (2009)."Education 2.0: The case for interactive whiteboards." Instructor, Vol. 118 n6, pp. 29-33.

Davis, B. G. (1993). Tools for Teaching. San Francisco: Jossey-Bass.

Gardner, H. (2011). Frames of Mind: The Theory of Multiple Intelligences, 3rd ed. New York, NY: Basic Books.

Greive, D., Lesko, P.D. (2011). A Handbook for Adjunct/Part-time Faculty and Teachers of Adults, 7th ed. Ann Arbor, MI: Part-Time Press.

Hass, Michael & Osborn, Jan. (2007, August 13). "An emic view of student writing and the writing process." Across the Disciplines, 4. Retrieved June 18, 2018, from https://wac.colostate.edu/ATD/articles/hass_osborn2007.cfm.

Hewitt, Anne, and Forte, Andrea (2006). Crossing Boundaries: Identity Management and Student/Faculty Relationships on the Facebook. Poster presented at CSCW Banff, Alberta.

Jaschik, Scott, and Lederman, Doug (2016). "Faculty Attitudes on Technology." InsideHigherEd.

(P. A. Kirschner and P. D. Bruyckere Teach. Teach. Educ. 67, 135–142; 2017)

Knowles, M. (1998). The Adult Learner: A Neglected Species. Houston, TX: Gulf.

Kowalski, R. M. (2003). Complaining, teasing, and other annoying behaviors. New Haven, CT: Yale University Press.

Kvavik, Robert B. (2016). "Convenience, Communications and Control: How Students Use Technology." Educating the Net Generation. Washington, DC: EDUCAUSE.

Lewis, Bryan & Starsia, Gerald (2009). "Challenges in Technology Implementation for Learning Spaces in Higher Education." EDUCAUSE Quarterly Magazine, Vol. 32 n1.

McKeachie, W. J. (2014). Teaching Tips, 14th Ed. Boston, MA: Cengage Learning.

Miller, Thomas E. (2007) "Will They Stay or Will They Go?: Predicting the Risk of Attrition at a Large Public University."

College & University, Vol. 83 n2 pp. 2-4, 6-7.

Nauert PhD, R. (2015). Updated Maslow's Pyramid of Needs. Psych Central. Retrieved on June 19, 2018, from https://psychcentral.com/news/2010/08/23/updated-maslows-pyramid-of-needs/17144.html

Perrin, Andrew (2015). "Social Media Usage: 2005-2015." Pew Research Center, Internet and Technology: Retrieved June 25, 2018, from http://www.pewinternet.org/2015/10/08/social-networking-usage-2005-2015/.

Prensky, Marc (2001). "Digital Natives, Digital Immigrants Part 1." On the Horizon, Vol. 9, Issue 5.

Quashie, Valerie (2009). "How Interactive is the Interactive Whiteboard." Mathematics Teaching, May 2009, pp.33-38.

Sego, A. (1998). Cooperative Learning: Professional's Guide. Westminster, CA: Teacher Created Materials.

Sorcinelli, Mary Deane (2002). "New conceptions of scholarship for a new generation of faculty members." New Directions for Teaching and Learning, Vol. 2002, Issue 90, pp. 41-48. San Francisco, CA: Jossey-Bass.

Strader, Reed, Suh & Njoroge (2016). "Acceptability of Social Media Use in Out-of-Class Faculty-Student Engagement." International Journal of Cyber Ethics in Education, Vol. 4 n2, pp. 22-40.

Thompson et al., (2013). A.A. Thompson, M.A. Peteraf, J.E. Gamble, A.J. Strickland, A. Janes, A. Sutton. Crafting and executing strategy: The quest for competitive advantage concepts and cases. McGraw Hill, Berkshire.

& Techniques

<u>Part-Time Press Instructional Products</u>

Teaching Strategies and Techniques, 6th Ed. *by Donald Greive,*

1-9 copies $15.00 each
10-49 copies 10% discount
50-99 copies 20% discount
100+ copies 30% discount

Blended Learning & Flipped Classrooms: A Comprehensive Guide *by Patricia Adams and Happy Gingras*

1-9 copies $15.00 each
10-49 copies 10% discount
50-99 copies 20% discount
100+ copies 30% discount

Handbook II: Advanced Teaching Strategies for Adjunct & PT Faculty *by P.D. Lesko and Donald Greive, Editors*

1-9 copies $20.00 each
10-49 copies 10% discount
50-99 copies 20% discount
100+ copies 30% discount

Order securely online at www.Part-TimePress.com
Order by phone: 734-930-6854/ Email orders@Part-TimePress.com

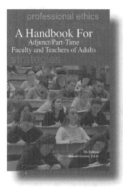

Handbook for Adjunct/Part-Time Faculty, 7th Edition *by Donald Greive*

1-9 copies $20.00 each
10-49 copies 10% discount
50-99 copies 20% discount
100+ copies 30% discount

Going the Distance: A Handbook for PT & Adjunct Faculty Who Teach Online, Rev. 1st Ed. *by Evelyn Beck*

1-9 copies $15.00 each
10-49 copies 10% discount
50-99 copies 20% discount
100+ copies 30% discount

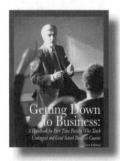

Getting Down to Business
by Dr. Bruce Johnson

1-9 copies $20.00 each
10-49 copies 10% discount
50-99 copies 20% discount
100+ copies 30% discount

Teaching in the Sciences: A Handbook for PT & Adjunct Faculty *by Dr. Michael Collins*

1-9 copies $15.00 each
10-49 copies 10% discount
50-99 copies 20% discount
100+ copies 30% discount

Part-Time Press Order Form

Qty	Title	Price
	Subtotal	
	Shipping	
	Total	

Purchaser/Payment Information

☐ *Check (payable to Part-Time Press)*

☐ *Credit Card # _____*

   Exp. Date _____ 3-digit CVV # _____

☐ *Purchase Order # _____*

Name _____

Title _____

Institution _____

Address _____

City/ST/Zip _____

Phone: _____ Fax: _____

Email: _____

Shipping Fee Schedule:

1-4 books $6.00
5+ books   8 percent of order subtotal

Order securely online at www.Part-TimePress.com
Order by phone: 734-930-6854/Email orders@Part-TimePress.com

Teaching Strategies